SOUP AND STEW COOKING

Edited by Jane Solmson

WEATHERVANE
BOOKS

Contents

Introduction

Everyone likes a bowl of steaming hot vegetable soup or a hearty helping of chunky beef stew on a cold and windy day. But why not learn how to make over 100 different kinds of soups and stews for every occasion from snowy day lunches to fancy dinner parties?

Soups and Stews explains how to make such old-time favorites as Irish stew and New England clam chowder, as well as venison stew and the chicken soup that's good for what ails you. Starting with the most basic soup stocks, this full-color cookbook shows you how easy it is to make leftovers into quick soups and stews that look and taste like you've slaved over a hot stove all day.

The key to soups and stews is variety. They can be main dishes accompanied only by a salad. Soups can be spiced and chilled. Stews can be made with luscious combinations of vegetables, seafoods and meats. *Soups and Stews* is guaranteed to tantalize the most finicky tastebuds with numerous special recipes of "unusual" soups. These intriguing recipes supply the perfect opportunity to test your imagination with dishes that have been called simple and boring—until now.

SOUPS

beef stock

3 pounds beef brisket
2 pounds medium soup
   bones
5 quarts water
4 green onions and tops

1 large onion, studded
   with 10 cloves
1 celery stalk and leaves
1 Bouquet Garni (see
   Index) (optional)
2 tablespoons salt

Place beef and bones in large baking pan. Bake at 400°F about 1 hour or until well-browned on both sides. Remove from pan; place in a large stockpot.

Drain off fat from baking pan; add 1 cup water to pan and scrape up brown bits from bottom. Pour into stockpot. Add remaining water and remaining ingredients except salt. Bring slowly to a boil, removing scum as it accumulates on surface. Cover and simmer 1 hour. Add salt. Simmer 3 hours longer.

Remove meat and vegetables. Strain through wet muslin. Chill; remove fat before using.

chicken stock

1 4-pound hen
1 pound chicken wings
2 tablespoons salt
4 peppercorns
5 quarts water
½ bay leaf
Pinch of thyme

6 green onions with tops
4 large carrots, quartered
2 stalks celery with leaves,
   cut in 2-inch pieces
1 large onion, studded
   with 3 cloves

Place chicken, salt, peppercorns and water in a stockpot. Bring to a boil over medium heat, removing scum from surface. Cover pot; reduce heat. Simmer 1 hour, skimming frequently. Add remaining ingredients; cover and cook about 2 hours and 30 minutes.

Skim off fat; season to taste with additional salt and pepper. Remove chicken and vegetables from stock. Strain stock through wet muslin. Chill and remove fat before using.

brown stock

2 to 3 pounds veal bones
2 to 3 pounds meaty
   beef bones (including
   a bone with marrow)
2 pounds of lean beef, in
   one piece for boiled
   beef or cut into pieces
3 to 4 onions, unpeeled,
   or 2 onions and 2 leeks
4 carrots

5 quarts water
10 peppercorns
2 bay leaves
8 to 10 sprigs of parsley
1 sprig of thyme (or ¼
   teaspoon dried thyme)
Salt and pepper
A few mushroom stalks
   or peelings

Get butcher to break bones. Put them into a pan with beef and a little beef marrow or good dripping. Heat pan; as the bones and meat brown, stir and keep from burning. Remove; keep warm while browning the vegetables. Return bones and meat to pan; cover with water. Add herbs, salt, pepper, and mushroom peelings or stems if available.

Bring to a boil. Skim frequently during the first hour. Then cover pan; simmer for 2 to 3 hours, by which time the stock should be well flavored and a good brown color. (If meat is a large piece and is to be used as boiled beef, this can be removed after 2 hours and stock simmered without it for remaining cooking time.)

Strain the stock; let cool. Then skim off fat, which will form a crust on top. If stock is not required for a day or two, do not remove fat until just before using, as it acts as a protective seal. Keep in a refrigerator or deep-freeze.

vegetable stock

3 medium onions,
   unpeeled
3 medium carrots, peeled
2 leeks, white part only
4 to 5 stalks of celery
1 small turnip, peeled
1 tablespoon butter or
   oil

2 to 3 quarts water
6 peppercorns
1 bay leaf
4 to 6 sprigs of parsley
1 sprig of thyme (or ¼
   teaspoon dried thyme)
Salt and pepper

Cut up vegetables; brown these until golden in either a little butter or oil. Add water, herbs and seasoning. Bring to a boil; simmer for 1½ to 2 hours, by which time the stock should be well flavored. Strain; cool. Use for soups or sauces calling for vegetable stock.

fish stock

½ to 1 pound fish back-
   bones and skins
1 onion, sliced
2 small carrots, sliced
2 stalks celery
6 sprigs of parsley

1 bay leaf
1 sprig of thyme
6 to 7 cups water
1½ cups white wine or
   cider (optional)
Salt and pepper

Use backbones from whitefish (sole, turbot or halibut preferably) and the skins if available. Put in a pan with sliced onion, carrot, celery, herbs and water. Add white wine or cider if available. Then add salt and pepper. Bring very slowly to a boil; simmer for 30 to 40 minutes, until liquid has reduced and is well flavored. Strain; cool. Use at once or freeze for later use.

white stock

2 pounds raw veal
    knuckle bones
1 chicken carcass and
    giblets
2 onions, peeled and
    sliced
2 carrots, peeled and
    sliced
3 stalks of celery
1 bay leaf

6 sprigs of parsley
1 small sprig of thyme
    (or ¼ teaspoon dried
    thyme)
2 teaspoons salt
6 peppercorns
1 small piece of mace
3 quarts water
Rind of ½ lemon

Have butcher chop raw veal bones and chicken carcass into small pieces. Put these and giblets into pan of water with vegetables, herbs and seasoning. Bring to a boil; skim frequently for about half an hour. Add 1 cup cold water; skim again. Add lemon rind; simmer 2 hours.

Strain through muslin and sieve. Then let cool. Remove fat from the top. Use at once, keep in covered bowl in refrigerator or freeze.

bouquet garni

1 parsley stalk
1 bay leaf
2 sprigs of thyme

1 sprig of marjoram
    (optional)

Combine all ingredients in a small piece of muslin or a double thickness of cheesecloth; tie securely with string.

fried bread croutons

2 large slices white
    bread
Oil
1 tablespoon butter

Salt and pepper
Onion powder to taste

Remove crusts from slices of bread; cut bread into small cubes. Heat enough oil in frying pan to come at least half way up the sides of bread cubes while cooking. When the oil is hot, add butter. When melted and foaming, add all bread cubes at once. Cook over a moderate-to-hot flame; stir constantly to ensure that cubes brown evenly. When golden brown, place on kitchen paper to drain. Remove from pan when slightly less brown than final color you want, as they continue to cook for a few seconds, because of hot oil.

Season with salt and pepper, and onion powder, if this will improve soup for which croutons are intended. Keep hot and serve separately. Serves 4.

bacon croutons

2 slices bacon
Oil

2 large slices white
    bread, cut into cubes
Pepper

Remove rinds from bacon slices; chop the bacon finely. Put into a dry frying pan; cook slowly to extract fat, then cook until crisp and golden. Remove bacon bits; reserve.

Add enough oil to bacon fat to cook diced bread in same way as Fried Bread Croutons. When golden brown, remove; drain. Add bacon bits with pepper and serve hot. Serves 4.

cheese croutons

2 to 3 slices white bread
2 tablespoons butter
  (approximately)
A little mustard or
  vegetable extract

4 to 6 tablespoons
  grated Italian cheese
Salt and pepper
Cayenne pepper

Toast bread slices on one side only. Let cool. Then butter reverse side; spread with a little mustard. Sprinkle thickly with grated cheese and a little salt and pepper. Broil until cheese is melted and browned. Sprinkle with cayenne pepper. When slightly cooled, cut into squares or fingers. Serve hot. Serves 4.

chicken noodle soup

4 to 5 cups well-flavored
  clear chicken stock (or
  water and cubes)
4 tablespoons fine noodles

Seasoning to taste
2 tablespoons finely
  chopped parsley

Bring stock to a boil; add noodles, stirring constantly; boil slowly about 15 minutes or for time stated on package of noodles. Stir frequently to prevent noodles from sticking. Season to taste. Serve hot in soup cups liberally sprinkled with finely chopped parsley. Serves 4 to 6.

chicken giblet soup

2 sets chicken giblets
1 large onion
2 to 3 carrots
2 to 3 stalks celery
Chicken skin and
  carcass (if available)
5 cups water

4 to 5 parsley stalks, 1
  sprig of thyme, 1 bay
  leaf, tied together
6 peppercorns
Salt
Chicken cube (optional)
2 tablespoons butter
1½ tablespoons flour

garnish
2 chicken livers
1 tablespoon butter

2 tablespoons chopped
  parsley

Wash chicken giblets, removing livers. Reserve for garnish.

Peel onion; slice onion, carrots and celery. Put into pan with giblets—and any skin or carcass from the chicken. Add water, herbs, peppercorns and some salt. Bring slowly to a boil, skimming off any scum that rises to top. Reduce heat and simmer 1 to 1½ hours, until the vegetables are tender and giblets well cooked. Taste soup; if not well flavored, a chicken cube can be added. (Remove skin and carcass, or strain soup into another pan.)

Melt 2 tablespoons butter; blend in flour. Strain onto chicken stock; blend thoroughly; bring to boil, stirring constantly. Cook few minutes.

Cook chicken livers gently in 1 tablespoon butter 5 to 8 minutes, depending on their size. Chop livers roughly; divide between soup cups before pouring on hot soup. Sprinkle with chopped parsley. Serves 4 to 6.

chicken gumbo

3 tablespoons butter or
  bacon fat
1 large or 2 smaller
  onions, chopped
1½ cups canned
  tomatoes, chopped
½ green pepper, seeded
  and chopped
¾ to 1 cup canned okra
  (or ready-cooked okra)
2 tablespoons rice

4 to 5 cups strongly
  flavored chicken stock
  made with whole
  chicken
1 to 2 cups chopped
  cooked chicken
1 tablespoon chopped
  parsley
1 teaspoon chopped
  tarragon
½ cup cooked corn
  (optional)

garnish
Fried Bread Croutons
  (see Index)

Melt butter or bacon fat in a soup pot; cook onion gently 5 to 6 minutes with lid on, until tender but not brown. Add chopped tomatoes, chopped pepper, okra and rice. Pour in stock; mix thoroughly. Add salt and pepper if necessary. Cover pan; simmer until the vegetables are tender, about 20 to 30 minutes.

Adjust seasoning; add chopped cooked chicken and herbs. If available, ½ cup of cooked corn can also be added. Reheat; serve hot. This soup can be served on its own as a main course; it is nice to serve Fried Bread Croutons (see Index) or thick bread and butter with it. Serves 4 to 6.

turkey and chestnut soup

3 to 4 tablespoons or
  more of leftover chest-
  nut stuffing (or 5 to 6
  tablespoons canned
  chestnut puree)
Carcass of one cooked
  turkey
2 onions, sliced
2 to 3 carrots, sliced

2 to 3 stalks of celery,
  sliced
Several sprigs of parsley
1 bay leaf
5 to 6 cups water
Salt and pepper
1 tablespoon butter
¾ tablespoon all-
  purpose flour

garnish
5 to 6 chestnuts
1 tablespoon chopped parsley

Remove remaining chestnut stuffing from cold turkey; reserve. Take off any pieces of turkey meat which can be used as a garnish. Break up turkey carcass; put into a large pan with sliced onions, carrots, celery and herbs. Cover with water; simmer until well flavored. Avoid boiling hard; this makes stock cloudy. Strain.

Put chestnut stuffing into electric blender with a cup of turkey stock; blend until smooth. Turn into a pan; add remaining 4 cups stock, seasoning and turkey meat. Cook together for a few minutes. If the soup is too thin, blend butter and flour together to make a paste; add to the soup in small pieces; stir until thickened. Bring to a boil; serve hot with a few cooked chestnuts, fried in butter, broken into pieces, and sprinkled on top with chopped parsley. Serves 4 to 6.

two-bean soup

1¼ cups dry white beans
¼ pound ham, cubed
1 cup cut green beans,
   fresh or frozen
¼ cup diced celery
1 green onion, diced
1 yellow onion, diced
1 potato, peeled and diced

1 tablespoon butter
2 tablespoons flour
¾ cup beef broth
½ teaspoon salt
¼ teaspoon pepper
1 sprig parsley for
   garnish

Cover white beans with cold water; soak overnight. Drain; place beans in a 2-quart saucepan. Add ham and enough cold water to cover beans by 1 inch. Bring water to a boil and simmer about 1 hour or until beans are tender. Add green beans, celery, onions, and potato. Add enough water to cover vegetables; simmer 20 minutes.

In a frypan melt butter; stir in flour. Cook, stirring, until lightly browned. Remove from heat; stir in heated beef broth. Cook mixture until smooth. Stir mixture into soup; simmer until soup is thickened and vegetables are tender. Season with salt and pepper. Garnish with chopped parsley; serve immediately. Serves 4 to 6.

green bean soup

2 to 3 tablespoons
   butter
1 medium onion (or 3 to
   4 shallots) finely
   chopped
1 clove garlic, crushed
2 tablespoons flour

4 cups chicken or veal
   stock
Salt and pepper
1 pound green beans
1 teaspoon chopped or
   dried summer savory
A little green coloring if
   required

garnish
4 to 6 tablespoons
   whipping cream
2 slices bacon

Melt butter; cook onion and garlic for 5 to 6 minutes in a covered pan. Add flour; blend in smoothly. Pour on stock; mix well. When smooth, bring to a boil, stirring constantly. Add salt and pepper.

String beans; cut in slanting slices or break in half depending on their size. Add to soup, with dried savory; cook for 25 minutes or until beans are tender.

Strain soup, reserving a few pieces of bean for garnish (keep warm). Put remaining soup and beans through a food mill or blend until smooth in electric blender.

Reheat soup; adjust seasoning to taste; add a little green coloring if required.

Serve hot with a spoon of whipped cream on each cup; sprinkle with finely crumbled crispy fried bacon. Serves 4 to 6.

lentil soup

lentil soup

2 cups lentils
8 cups water
½ cup chopped onion
2 cloves garlic, minced
½ cup chopped carrots
½ cup chopped celery
¼ cup olive oil
1 teaspoon salt
½ teaspoon pepper
3 tablespoons tomato
  paste
2 bay leaves
½ teaspoon oregano
3 tablespoons wine
  vinegar

Wash and pick over lentils. Soak them overnight in 2 cups of water. In a Dutch oven or soup kettle sauté onion, garlic, carrot, and celery in olive oil. Add lentils, 6 cups of water, salt, pepper, tomato paste, bay leaves, and oregano. Bring to a boil; cook 2½ to 3 hours or until the lentils are soft. Remove bay leaves.

At this point mixture may be pureed in the blender until smooth. Thin with water if necessary.

Return mixture to the soup pot; heat. Add wine vinegar; serve. Serves 6 to 8.

clear tomato soup

clear tomato soup

1 pound very ripe tomatoes	1 teaspoon dried basil
	1 teaspoon salt
3 pints Chicken Stock (see Index)	$^1/_8$ teaspoon white pepper

Cut tomatoes in large chunks; place in small saucepan. Add ½ cup stock and basil. Simmer 20 minutes.

Force tomato mixture through a sieve into a bowl. Let set for several minutes.

Pour remaining stock in a medium saucepan; add tomato mixture except sediment in bottom of bowl. Add salt and pepper. Simmer until soup is reduced to about 2 pints. Float a basil leaf on top if available. Serves 4 to 6.

fresh mushroom soup

1 pound fresh mushrooms	4 cups chicken broth or bouillon
2 tablespoons vegetable oil	¼ teaspoon salt
2 scallions or shallots, minced	½ teaspoon lemon juice
	1 lemon, sliced

Wash mushrooms; pat dry with paper towels. Chop very fine or chop small amounts at a time in blender on slowest speed.

Heat oil in frypan and sauté scallions about 3 minutes or until wilted. Add mushrooms; cook, stirring occasionally, about 5 minutes. Add broth, salt, and lemon juice. Bring to a boil. Reduce heat to a simmer and cook uncovered 30 minutes.

Blend finished soup in blender or press through a coarse sieve. If sieved, press hard on mushrooms to extract all liquid. Reheat before serving. Garnish with lemon slices. Serves 6.

onion soup

onion soup

4 large onions, thinly
  sliced
1 tablespoon butter
1 tablespoon vegetable
  oil
¼ teaspoon sugar
2 tablespoons flour
6 cups beef broth
¼ cup dry white wine or
  vermouth

Salt and pepper to taste
4 slices French bread,
  cut ½ inch thick
2 teaspoons vegetable
  oil
1 clove garlic, peeled
  and cut
2 tablespoons cognac
1 cup grated Swiss
  cheese

In covered 4-quart saucepan or Dutch oven cook onions slowly
with butter and 1 tablespoon oil 15 minutes. Stir occasionally.
Uncover; increase heat to moderate. Add sugar; sauté onions, stirring frequently, about 30 minutes or until onions turn golden
brown. Sprinkle onions with flour; stir over heat 2 to 3 minutes.
Blend in hot broth and wine; adjust seasonings. Simmer, partially
covered, 1 hour.

Meanwhile, place bread slices in 350°F oven 30 minutes or until
lightly toasted. Halfway through baking, baste each slice with ½
teaspoon oil; rub with cut garlic clove.

Before serving, add cognac; divide soup into ovenproof bowls or
casseroles. Sprinkle ½ cup cheese in soup. Float slices of French
bread on top of soup; sprinkle with rest of cheese.

Bake in preheated 325°F oven 15 to 20 minutes, until hot, then
set under broiler 2 to 3 minutes, until cheese is golden brown.
Serve immediately. Serves 4.

13

neopolitan minestrone

1½ pounds beef shanks
1 onion, quartered
1 package soup greens
(or 2 celery stalks, 1
carrot, 1 potato, 1
turnip and a sprig of
parsley, all cleaned
and chopped)
1 small bay leaf
2 whole peppercorns
1 clove

1½ teaspoons salt
6 cups water
1 celery root
¼ pound ham
2 ounces penne or elbow
macaroni
3 tablespoons tomato
paste
1 teaspoon dry chervil
4 tablespoons grated
Parmesan cheese

neopolitan minestrone

In a large Dutch oven, combine beef shanks, onion, soup greens, bay leaf, peppercorns, clove, and salt. Add water; bring to a boil. Skim any foam. Reduce the heat to low; simmer covered 1½ to 2 hours. Remove meat; cool. Strain broth; skim fat. Return broth to pot. Clean celery root and cut into thin sticks. Dice meat from beef shanks; cut ham into thin strips.

Boil macaroni until tender in boiling salted water; drain. Bring broth to a boil. Combine tomato paste with 1 cup of broth; stir until dissolved. Add to broth in pot along with celery root, diced beef and ham. Cover; cook 15 minutes. Add macaroni and chervil; heat through.

Sprinkle with Parmesan cheese; serve. Serves 6.

14

carrot soup

3 cups Chicken Stock
  (see Index)
1 small onion, chopped
4 carrots, peeled and
  sliced
1/8 teaspoon nutmeg

2 tablespoons peanut
  butter
1 tablespoon Worcester-
  shire sauce
1 clove garlic, minced
Dash of Tabasco sauce

Simmer together all ingredients until tender, about 15 minutes.
Remove half of carrots. Puree rest of ingredients.

Add reserved carrots; reheat before serving. Garnish with chopped
peanuts, apples and green onions. Serves 4.

parsnip soup

3 tablespoons butter
1 onion, chopped
1½ cups peeled and
  finely sliced parsnips
1 tablespoon flour
3 to 4 cups Vegetable or
  White Stock (see
  Index) (or water and
  cube)

3 to 4 sprigs of parsley
1 small bay leaf
A pinch of thyme
A pinch of nutmeg
Salt and pepper
½ cup cream

garnish
1 tablespoon chopped
  parsley
Fried Bread Croutons
  (see Index)

Melt butter; cook onion and parsnips gently 5 to 6 minutes with a
lid on pan, to soften without browning. Remove from heat; sprinkle
in flour. Then blend well. Pour on stock; mix well; add herbs and
seasonings. Bring to a boil; simmer 20 to 30 minutes, until
parsnips are tender. Remove bay leaf.

Put soup into electric blender; blend until smooth; or put through
food mill. Return soup to pan; adjust seasoning; reheat, adding
cream.

Serve in soup cups sprinkled with chopped parsely and with Fried
Bread Croutons. Serves 4.

ham chowder

2 cups potatoes, pared,
  diced
¼ cup celery, chopped
  very fine
¼ cup onion, chopped
  very fine
1 teaspoon salt

1½ cups boiling water
3 cups milk
1½ cups ham, finely
  chopped
¼ cup unsifted flour
¼ cup water

Cook potatoes, celery, and onion in boiling salted water until
tender.

Add milk and ham. Heat to simmering.

Mix flour and ¼ cup water. Stir into milk mixture.

Cook, stirring occasionally, until thickened. Serves 6.

1 small green cabbage
    (or 2 cups of shredded
    green cabbage)
2 slices fat bacon
1 large onion, chopped
2 small leeks, white part
    only, sliced
2 carrots, sliced
1 potato, sliced
1 tablespoon flour

4 cups Brown Stock (see
    Index) (or water and
    cubes; ham stock can
    be used, if not too
    salty)
2 tablespoons chopped
    parsley
1 bay leaf
Salt and pepper
A pinch of nutmeg
2 teaspoons chopped dill
    or 1 teaspoon dillseeds

garnish
Fat for frying
3 to 4 frankfurters

Slice and wash green cabbage; put into a pan of boiling salted water; cook 5 minutes. Drain and rinse under cold water.

Meanwhile, chop bacon; heat over gentle heat until fat runs. Add onion, leeks, carrots and potato; stir over heat a few minutes. Sprinkle in flour; blend well before adding stock (or water and cubes). Add parsley, bay leaf, salt and pepper. Bring to a boil. Reduce heat; simmer 10 minutes before adding cabbage. Cook 20 minutes more, or until vegetables are tender but not mushy.

Adjust seasoning; add nutmeg and chopped dill, or a few dillseeds. Remove bay leaf.

For garnish, fry frankfurters and cut in slices, putting a few slices into each serving. Serves 4 to 6.

2 pounds fresh spinach
    or 2 packages frozen
    chopped spinach
2 quarts Chicken Stock
    (see Index)
3 tablespoons butter
2 tablespoons flour

1 teaspoon salt
Dash of freshly ground
    pepper
1/8 teaspoon nutmeg
Hard-cooked egg for
    garnish (optional)

Thoroughly wash spinach, then drain it. Chop it coarsely. If frozen spinach is used, thaw it completely and drain it.

Bring soup stock to a boil in a 4-quart pot; add spinach. Simmer it uncovered about 8 minutes. Strain spinach from stock into separate bowls. Press spinach with a spoon to remove most liquid. If desired, chop cooked spinach even finer.

Melt butter in soup pot, then remove it from heat. Stir in flour, being careful to avoid lumps. Add liquid stock, 1 cup at a time, stirring constantly. Return it to heat; bring it to a boil. Add spinach, salt, pepper, and nutmeg. The soup will thicken slightly. Simmer about 5 minutes more.

Serve soup, garnishing each serving with a few slices of hard-cooked egg, if desired. Serves 4 to 6.

spring soup

4 young carrots
2 to 3 young leeks,
   according to size (or 8
   to 10 scallions)
3 tablespoons butter
1½ tablespoons flour
4 cups Chicken Stock
   (see Index) (or water
   and chicken cubes)
½ cup cauliflower florets

2 to 3 tablespoons peas
2 to 3 tablespoons
   young green beans,
   sliced
A little sugar
2 tablespoons mixed
   parsley, chervil, mint
   and thyme
Salt and pepper

liaison
½ cup cream
2 egg yolks

Peel and dice carrots. Wash leeks or scallions thoroughly; cut white part into slices. Melt butter; cook these vegetables gently in a covered pan 5 to 6 minutes without allowing to brown. Sprinkle in flour, mix thoroughly, then add stock. Blend well until smooth; bring to a boil, stirring constantly. Cook a few minutes before adding cauliflower florets, peas, sliced beans and sugar. Simmer 15 minutes. Add herbs; cook a few more minutes, to draw out flavor of herbs. Season to taste.

Make liaison by mixing cream with egg yolks. Take a few spoonfuls of hot soup; mix well with cream and egg-yolk mixture before straining it back into soup, stirring constantly. Reheat, being very careful not to allow soup to boil, as this causes egg to curdle and spoils texture of soup. Serves 4 to 6.

hearty vegetable soup

1 cup cooked beef, cut
   in small pieces
6 cups beef broth
2 cups fresh or canned
   tomatoes
1 cup diced potatoes
¾ cup diced carrots
½ cup sliced onion

3 cups other uncooked
   vegetables (green peas,
   chopped cabbage, diced
   celery, cut green beans,
   chopped green pepper,
   sliced okra, diced
   turnips, cut corn)
1½ teaspoons salt
⅛ teaspoon pepper

Combine beef and broth in a large saucepan. Add remaining ingredients.

Cook, covered, about 35 minutes, or until vegetables are tender. Serves 6.

notes
In place of beef broth use 6 beef bouillon cubes and 6 cups water. (Liquid from canned or cooked vegetables may replace some of the water.)

Canned or leftover vegetables may be used instead of uncooked vegetables. Add to soup during last few minutes of cooking.

potato soup

2 tablespoons margarine
2 tablespoons finely
   chopped onion
1 cup diced potato
4 tablespoons water
½ clove garlic, crushed

Salt and pepper
1 cup milk
1 tablespoon chopped
   parsley
A pinch of nutmeg

Heat margarine in a pan; add onion and potato; sauté about 5 minutes.

Add water, garlic and a little salt and pepper. Cover; cook over low heat until potato is quite soft.

Add milk; stir until soup boils. Then mash through a sieve.

Return to pan; adjust seasoning; add parsley and a pinch of nutmeg; reheat before serving. Serves 3 to 4.

watercress soup

2 bunches fresh
   watercress
3 tablespoons butter
1 potato, sliced
1 small onion, finely
   chopped
1 tablespoon flour
3 cups White or Chicken
   Stock (see Index) (or
   water)

3 to 4 sprigs of parsley
1 bay leaf
Salt and pepper
2 cups milk
¼ teaspoon mace
A little green coloring
   (optional)

garnish
4 to 6 tablespoons
   cream
Watercress sprigs
Fried Bread Croutons
   (see Index)

Wash and pick over watercress, discarding any yellow leaves. Reserve enough green top-sprigs to make final garnish; chop remaining cress roughly. Melt butter; cook potato and onion together 2 to 3 minutes before adding chopped watercress. Continue cooking 3 to 4 minutes, stirring constantly to prevent browning. Sprinkle in flour; blend well. Add stock; blend together before bringing to a boil. Add herbs and some seasoning; reduce heat; simmer until potato is tender, about 20 minutes.

Remove bay leaf. Put soup into electric blender; blend until smooth, or put through fine food mill or sieve. Return soup to pan; reheat gently. At same time heat milk in a separate pan. When almost at boiling point, pour into watercress mixture (this makes texture of soup lighter and more delicate). Adjust seasoning, adding mace and a little green coloring if desired.

Serve with a spoon of cream in each cup and reserved watercress sprigs on top. Fried Bread Croutons are also excellent with this soup. Serves 4 to 6.

18

pavian soup

4 slices white bread
3 tablespoons melted
   butter
5 cups Chicken Stock
   (see Index) *or* 2
   13-ounce cans regular
   strength chicken broth
4 eggs
6 tablespoons shredded
   Parmesan cheese

Trim crusts from bread. Brush on both sides with melted butter; place on a cookie sheet. Bake at 350°F 30 minutes, or until golden. Pour stock into a large shallow saucepan; heat to boiling.

Reduce heat to low, then break eggs one at a time into a saucer; slide into liquid. Poach lightly. Remove with a slotted spoon and keep warm. Strain stock; return to pan; heat to boiling. Put one toasted bread slice in each soup bowl. Top with 1 poached egg. Ladle soup over egg.

Sprinkle each bowl with 1½ tablespoons of cheese and serve. Serves 4.

pavian soup

oriental soup

1 quart chicken broth
½ cup bamboo shoots,
   cut into thin strips
2 ounces whole, cooked
   shrimps
½ pound cooked lean pork,
   cut into thin strips

2 ounces cooked
   chicken, cut into thin
   strips
½ teaspoon salt
¼ teaspoon soy sauce

Heat the chicken broth and add the remaining ingredients. Simmer for 3 to 4 minutes or until ingredients are hot. Serves 4 to 6.

oriental soup

meat dumplings
2 slices bread
½ pound lean ground beef

Salt
White pepper
5 cups beef bouillon

soup
¼ head savoy cabbage (green cabbage can be substituted), sliced
1 leek, sliced
2 ounces fresh mushrooms, sliced
1 celery stalk, sliced
1 tablespoon oil

1 small onion, chopped
2 ounces frozen peas
4 ounces egg noodles
Salt and white pepper
1 tablespoon soy sauce
3 tablespoons sherry

Soak bread in small amount of cold water. Squeeze as dry as possible; mix with ground beef and salt and pepper to taste. Bring bouillon to a boil. Using 1 teaspoon of meat mixture, form little dumplings; drop into boiling broth. Reduce heat; simmer 10 minutes.

For soup, slice cabbage, leek, mushrooms and celery. Heat oil in a large saucepan. Add onion; cook until golden. Add sliced vegetables; cook 5 minutes. Remove dumplings from beef broth with a slotted spoon; drain on paper toweling; keep warm. Strain broth; add to vegetables. Add peas and noodles; simmer 15 minutes. Return dumplings to soup. Season with salt, pepper, soy sauce and sherry. Serve immediately. Serves 4 to 6.

soup with vegetables and meat dumplings

greek lemon soup

greek lemon soup

2 quarts Chicken Stock
  (see Index)
⅓ cup long grain rice,
  rinsed
3 eggs, separated
2 tablespoons lemon
  juice

Pour stock into a 4-quart saucepan; bring to a boil. Reduce heat; simmer 5 to 10 minutes. Add rice; cook 15 to 20 minutes or until rice is tender. Remove from heat; cool slightly.

Beat egg yolks until thick and lemon colored, then add egg whites. Beat until foamy, adding lemon juice slowly and beating constantly.

Pour ½ cup of the broth into egg mixture very slowly, beating constantly to keep foamy, then beat in 1½ cups broth gradually. Pour egg mixture slowly into remaining broth in saucepan, stirring constantly. Reheat slowly but do not boil. Serve immediately. Serves 6.

beer and bread soup

1 small loaf dark rye
  bread
3 cups water
3 cups dark beer or ale
½ cup sugar

1 whole lemon (both
  juice and grated rind)
Light or whipped cream
  for garnish

Break bread in small pieces into a mixing bowl.

Mix water and beer; pour this over bread. Allow it to stand several hours.

When ready to serve, cook mixture over a low flame, stirring occasionally, just long enough for it to thicken. (If the mixture is too thick, strain it through a coarse sieve.) Bring it to a boil; add sugar, lemon juice, and lemon rind.

Serve soup with a spoonful of light or whipped cream on top. Serves 6 to 8.

1 medium onion,
  chopped
1 large carrot, chopped
1 tablespoon dry white
  wine
1 tablespoon water
3 cups hot beef bouillon
1 teaspoon sage
1 teaspoon tarragon

1 10-ounce package
  frozen peas
Salt and pepper to taste
12 ounces medium
  cooked shrimps,
  canned or frozen
½ cup white wine
¼ cup skim evaporated
  milk

savory shrimp soup

In a 4-quart saucepan or Dutch oven, cook onion and carrot in 1 tablespoon wine and water until onion is soft. Add bouillon; simmer 12 minutes. Add sage, tarragon, and green peas; bring to a boil; simmer 8 minutes.

Puree vegetable–bouillon mixture in a blender or food mill; return to pan. Season to taste with salt and pepper. Add shrimps; heat without boiling about 2 minutes. Stir in ½ cup white wine and the evaporated milk. Correct seasonings; serve immediately. Serves 4.

savory shrimp soup

maryland crab soup

6 cups strong Beef Stock
   (see Index)
3 cups mixed vegetables,
   fresh, leftover or
   frozen (include chopped
   onions and celery, diced
   carrots, peas, lima beans,
   cut string beans, corn,
   okra and tomatoes;
   not squash, cabbage
   or potatoes)
Seafood seasoning to
   taste
1 pound crab meat (claw
   or white meat)
Claws and pieces of
   whole crab if available
   (either raw or cooked)

Heat stock in a large soup pot. Add vegetables and seasoning; simmer 1 hour.

Add crab meat and crab claws and pieces (if available) 30 minutes before serving. Simmer gently, to heat through and allow flavors to blend.

Serve hot in large soup bowls, with bread and butter or hard crusty rolls and butter as accompaniment. Serves 4 to 6.

kidney soup

3 lamb kidneys or ½
   pound ox kidney
Salted water to cover
   kidneys for soaking
2 to 3 tablespoons
   butter or oil
2 onions, chopped
2 carrots, sliced
2 stalks celery, sliced
1½ tablespoons flour
1 tablespoon tomato
   puree
5 cups Beef or Brown
   Stock (see Index)
1 teaspoon Worcester-
   shire sauce
Several sprigs of parsley,
   1 sprig thyme, 1 bay
   leaf, tied together
Salt and pepper
1 cup sliced mushrooms
A dash of Tabasco or
   chili sauce
A little gravy mix, beef
   bouillon or soy sauce
2 to 3 tablespoons
   sherry
2 tablespoons chopped
   parsley

garnish
Fried Bread Croutons (see Index)

Remove skin and cores from kidneys; cut into small pieces. Soak a few minutes in cold, slightly salted water to remove any strong flavor. Drain.

Melt butter; cook the onions, carrots and celery for a few minutes, stirring well. Add kidney; cook 6 to 7 minutes to brown all ingredients lightly. Sprinkle in flour; mix well. Add tomato puree, stock and Worcestershire sauce. Bring to a boil slowly, stirring constantly. Add herbs and seasoning. Then cover pan; simmer about 45 minutes, until kidney and vegetables are tender. Remove herbs.

Just before end of cooking time, add sliced mushrooms and a dash of Tabasco or chili sauce. Adjust seasoning; if soup is not a good color, add a little gravy mix, beef bouillon or soy sauce.

Just before serving, add sherry and sprinkle with chopped parsley. Serve with fried croutons. Serves 4 to 6.

cold buttermilk soup

3 egg yolks
½ cup sugar
1 teaspoon lemon juice
½ teaspoon grated
  lemon rind
1 teaspoon vanilla
1 quart buttermilk

Beat egg yolks lightly in a large bowl, gradually adding sugar.

Add lemon juice, rind, and vanilla. Slowly add buttermilk, continuing to beat (either with an electric beater on slow or with a wire whisk) until soup is smooth.

Serve soup in chilled soup bowls. Serves 6 to 8.

cream of curry soup

3 tablespoons butter
1 large onion, chopped
1 sour cooking apple,
  peeled and cored
½ tablespoon curry
  powder or paste (or
  more if desired)
1 tablespoon flour
2 tablespoons rice
4 to 5 cups Chicken Stock
  (see Index) (or water
  and cubes)
1 teaspoon sweet
  chutney
2 teaspoons coconut
Salt and pepper
1 bay leaf
3 to 4 sprigs of parsley
1 slice lemon
½ cup cream

garnish
1 tablespoon chopped
  parsley (or paprika)
Lemon wedges
½ to 1 cup plain boiled
  rice

Melt butter; cook onion and apple gently 5 to 6 minutes to soften without browning. Stir in curry powder or paste; cook 1 minute. Remove from heat; sprinkle in flour. Blend well. Then add rice, stock, chutney and coconut. Bring to a boil, stirring constantly. Reduce heat. Add seasonings, herbs and slice of lemon. Cover pan; simmer 15 to 20 minutes to cook rice.

Remove bay leaf and lemon. Put soup into electric blender; blend until smooth. Reheat; adjust seasoning; just before serving, stir in cream.

Sprinkle with chopped parsley or paprika; serve lemon wedges and plain boiled rice separately. Serves 4 to 6.

vichyssoise

¾ pound leeks, halved
  lengthwise and sliced
  thinly
1 medium onion, chopped
2 tablespoons butter
2 large potatoes, peeled
  and diced

3 cups Chicken Stock
  (see Index)
Salt to taste
2 cups light cream
Dash Tabasco sauce
1 cup plain yogurt
Chopped chives

Heat leeks and onion in butter in a large skillet until transparent; do not brown. Add potatoes, chicken stock, and salt. Simmer until potatoes are tender, about 30 minutes.

Pour soup into blender; puree. Stir in cream and Tabasco sauce. Strain soup through a sieve; chill.

Just before serving, stir in yogurt. Readjust seasoning.

Serve soup very cold, garnished with chopped chives. Serves 6.

cream of corn soup

3 tablespoons butter
1 onion, chopped
1 medium potato, finely
  sliced
1½ cups fresh or canned
  corn
3½ cups milk
1 bay leaf
3 to 4 sprigs of parsley
Salt and pepper
¼ teaspoon mace
1 chicken stock cube

garnish
4 to 6 spoons heavy
  cream
1 tablespoon chopped
  chives or parsley (or a
  sprinkling of paprika)
Fried Bread Croutons
  (see Index)

Melt butter; cook onion and potato gently with lid on pan 5 minutes, shaking pan occasionally to prevent sticking. Add 1 cup corn. Stir well. Add milk, bay leaf, parsley, salt, pepper and mace. Bring to simmering heat; add a chicken stock cube; cook until vegetables are tender.

Put soup into electric blender; blend until smooth; or put through fine food mill.

Return soup to pan with remaining corn (which if fresh should be simmered until tender in salted water). Reheat soup until nearly boiling; adjust seasoning.

Serve in soup cups with a spoonful of cream in each cup, a sprinkling of chopped chives, parsley or paprika, and Fried Bread Croutons. Serves 4 to 6.

Picture on opposite page: vichyssoise

avocado soup

2 ripe, soft avocados,
  pitted and peeled
1 teaspoon lemon juice
1 cup cold chicken broth
1 cup light cream
½ cup plain yogurt
½ cup dry white wine
Salt to taste

Set aside a few thin slices of avocado brushed with lemon juice to use as a garnish. Place remaining avocado in a food processor or blender; blend until smooth.

Add remaining ingredients; blend until smooth.

Serve soup very cold, garnished with reserved avocado slices. Serves 4.

cold beet soup with sour cream

2 1-pound cans diced
  beets, drained
3 cups Beef Stock (see
  Index)
1 teaspoon wine vinegar
¼ cup Burgundy
1 tablespoon onion juice
¼ teaspoon white
  pepper
2 teaspoons celery salt
¼ cup orange juice
1 carton sour cream
1 tablespoon finely
  minced parsley

Combine half beets and a small amount of stock in a blender container; process until beets are pureed.

Repeat the process, using remaining beets and a small amount of stock. Combine pureed beets mixture, remaining stock, vinegar, Burgundy, onion juice, seasonings and orange juice; chill several hours.

Serve in individual soup bowls with a dollop of sour cream, sprinkled with parsley. Two pounds of fresh, cooked beets may be substituted for canned beets. Serves 8 to 10.

Picture on opposite page: avocado soup

cold beet soup with sour cream

cream of brussels sprout soup

4 tablespoons butter
1 onion, chopped
1 potato, chopped
4 cups washed and
    trimmed Brussels
    sprouts, chopped
1½ tablespoons flour

4 cups White Stock (see
    Index) (or water and
    chicken cubes)
2 bay leaves
3 to 4 sprigs of parsley
Salt and pepper
¼ teaspoon mace
1 cup light cream or milk

garnish

1 cup of cooked chest-
    nuts, broken into
    pieces

2 to 3 tablespoons
    butter

Melt butter; cook onion and potato 2 to 3 minutes. Then add chopped sprouts; cook 5 minutes, stirring constantly. Sprinkle in flour; blend well. Pour on stock. Stir until well mixed and smooth. Bring to a boil, stirring constantly. Reduce heat; add bay leaves, parsley sprigs and seasoning. Cover; simmer soup about 20 minutes, or until vegetables are tender but not overcooked, as this would give soup an unpleasant flavor.

Remove bay leaves. Put soup through food mill or into electric blender; blend until smooth. Adjust seasoning; reheat soup, adding at last moment a cup of hot cream or creamy milk.

Sprinkle with pieces of cooked chestnut, fried in butter until golden brown. Serves 4 to 6.

cream of mushroom soup

¼ cup butter
½ cup finely chopped
    onion
1 pound mushrooms
6 tablespoons flour
6 cups chicken broth
1 bay leaf
2 sprigs parsley
½ teaspoon salt
⅛ teaspoon pepper

2 tablespoons butter
1 tablespoon lemon
    juice
1 cup heavy cream or
    half-and-half
2 egg yolks
½ cup sour cream
Chopped parsley, if
    desired

Melt butter in 3-quart saucepan. Add onion and stems from mushrooms; cook until onion is tender. Stir in flour; add broth. Cook over medium heat, stirring constantly, until thickened. Add bay leaf, parsley sprigs, salt, and pepper. Simmer 20 minutes. Strain; return to pan.

In small frying pan sauté sliced mushroom caps in 2 tablespoons butter and lemon juice. Add to strained broth; simmer 10 minutes.

Blend cream and egg yolks. Slowly add small amount of soup to yolks, then add yolks to soup, stirring constantly. Heat gently 2 minutes. Stir in sour cream.

Serve soup hot. Garnish with chopped parsley. Serves 8.

cream of lettuce soup

1/4 cup butter
1 leek or green onion,
   chopped
1/2 cup chopped onion
1 quart shredded lettuce
4 tablespoons flour
1 tablespoon chopped
   parsley
1/2 teaspoon salt
1/8 teaspoon nutmeg
6 cups chicken broth
2 egg yolks
1/2 cup heavy cream
Lettuce and parsley for
   garnish

Melt butter in 3-quart saucepan. Add leek or onion; sauté until tender. Add lettuce; cover; simmer 5 minutes. Stir in flour. Add parsley and seasonings and chicken broth. Simmer gently 30 minutes. Puree soup in blender.

Mix egg yolks and cream in small bowl. Stir in 1/4 cup hot soup. Gradually add egg mixture to hot soup, stirring constantly. Heat gently several minutes, until soup thickens.

Garnish soup with shredded lettuce and parsley. Serves 8.

note
Use Boston Bibb or romaine lettuce for best flavor. Do not use iceberg (head) lettuce.

puree of turnip soup

3 tablespoons butter
2 cups sliced young
   turnips
1 cup sliced potatoes
1 small onion, sliced
1 1/2 tablespoons flour
3 cups White or Chicken
   Stock (see Index)
1 cup milk
1 tablespoon chopped
   parsley (or 1 teaspoon
   paprika)

garnish
Bacon Croutons (see
   Index)

Melt butter; cook turnips, potatoes and onion gently until they are tender, 20 to 30 minutes. Sprinkle in a little flour; blend thoroughly. Pour on stock; mix well before bringing to a boil. Reduce heat; simmer 15 minutes.

Put soup into electric blender; blend until smooth. Reheat, adding more seasoning, if necessary, and the milk.

Sprinkle with parsley or paprika on top; serve Bacon Croutons separately. Serves 4 to 6.

1 large freshly boiled
  lobster (or 2 small,
  preferably female,
  lobsters)
5 to 6 cups Fish Stock
  (see Index)
1 small onion, sliced
1 carrot, sliced
2 stalks celery, sliced
1 bay leaf, 3 to 4 sprigs
  of parsley, tied together

Salt and pepper
5 tablespoons butter
2½ tablespoons flour
¼ teaspoon mace or
  nutmeg
1 cup cream
3 to 4 tablespoons
  sherry (or brandy)
Paprika for garnish

Split freshly boiled lobster down back with a sharp knife; remove intestine, which looks like a long black thread down center of the back. Also remove stomach sac from head and tough gills. Crack claws, remove meat and add this to back meat. If lobster is female and there is red coral or roe, reserve this for garnish. Also reserve greenish curd from head.

Break up all lobster shells; put into a pan with fish stock. Add onion, carrot, celery, herbs, salt and pepper. Cover pan; simmer 30 to 45 minutes.

Meanwhile, cut lobster meat into chunks. Pound coral roe with 2 tablespoons butter to use as garnish and to color soup.

Melt 3 tablespoons butter in a pot; stir in flour until smoothly blended; cook a minute or two before adding strained lobster stock. Blend until smooth; then bring to a boil, stirring constantly. Reduce heat; simmer 4 to 5 minutes before adding lobster meat. Remove herbs. Add mace or nutmeg; adjust seasoning. Lastly, add cup of hot cream and the sherry (or brandy).

Serve in soup cups with a piece of the coral butter in each cup and sprinkle with paprika. Serves 6.

1 small ham hock
¾ cup split green peas
1 bay leaf
6 cups beef broth
6 slices bacon, diced
¾ cup chopped onion
1 stalk celery, diced
3 tablespoons flour

1 8-ounce can tomato
  puree
1 cup chicken broth
⅓ cup sherry
¼ cup butter
Freshly ground pepper
  to taste

Place ham hock, split peas, bay leaf, and 4 cups beef broth into 4-quart saucepan. Bring to a boil; reduce heat; simmer. Sauté bacon in frypan until fat is rendered. Add onion and celery; cook until tender. Stir in flour; mix to blend. Add remaining 2 cups beef broth; cook until slightly thickened. Add onion mixture to split-pea mixture; continue to cook until split peas are soft, about 1½ hours.

When done, remove ham hock. Puree mixture in blender or food mill. Add tomato puree, chicken broth, and sherry. Add butter and pepper; stir until melted.

Strain soup, if desired, before serving. Serves 8 to 12.

cheese and spinach soup

1/4 cup margarine
1 large onion, peeled
  and chopped
2 1/2 cups White Stock or
  Vegetable Stock (see
  Index) or water
1 cup milk
3 tablespoons flour
Salt and pepper
Nutmeg
2 teaspoons chopped
  parsley
1/2 cup grated cheese
4 tablespoons chopped
  cooked spinach
Few chives or scallions
Graham cracker crumbs

Heat fat in a kettle; add onion; sauté until translucent but not brown.

Add hot stock or water; simmer 10 minutes. Then add milk.

Mix flour to a smooth paste with a little extra milk; add gradually to the liquid in pan; stir until boiling.

Add salt, pepper and a little nutmeg to taste; stir over low heat 5 minutes.

Add parsley, cheese and spinach; bring to a boil again; adjust seasoning. Serve very hot with a sprinkling of chopped chives and crushed graham cracker crumbs. Serves 4.

creamy crab broccoli soup

1 package (6 to 8 ounces)
  frozen Alaska king crab,
  thawed, or 1 can (7 1/2
  ounces) Alaska king crab
1 package (10 ounces)
  frozen chopped
  broccoli
1/2 cup chopped onion
3 tablespoons butter or
  margarine

2 tablespoons flour
2 cups milk
2 cups half-and-half
2 chicken bouillon cubes
1/2 teaspoon salt
1/8 teaspoon black
  pepper
1/8 teaspoon cayenne
  pepper
1/4 teaspoon thyme

Drain and slice crab. Cook broccoli according to package directions. Sauté onion in butter or margarine. Blend in flour. Add milk and half-and-half, stirring and cooking until thickened and smooth.

Dissolve bouillon cubes in hot soup. Add seasonings, crab and broccoli; heat through. Serves 4 to 6.

russian sauerkraut soup

3 to 4 tablespoons
  butter
1 onion, sliced
2 small carrots, sliced
1 potato, peeled and
  sliced
2 tablespoons flour
1 teaspoon tomato puree

¾ pound sauerkraut
4 to 5 cups Brown Stock
  (see Index) or
  household stock
1 tablespoon chopped
  parsley
1 teaspoon chopped
  chervil

garnish
Sour cream

Melt butter; cook onion and carrots until golden. Then add potato.
Stir in flour; when smooth, add tomato puree and sauerkraut.
Cook a few minutes, stirring constantly. Then add stock and
herbs.

Bring to a boil; simmer about 40 minutes. Season to taste; serve
hot with a spoonful of sour cream in each soup cup. Serves 4
to 6.

sicilian sausage soup

¼ pound sweet Italian
  sausage (with the
  casing removed)
½ cup finely chopped
  onion
¼ cup chopped peeled
  carrots
¼ cup chopped celery
2 tablespoons chopped
  parsley
1 16-ounce can Italian-
  style peeled tomatoes,
  broken up with a fork
1 13¾-ounce can regular
  strength chicken broth
½ teaspoon dried sweet
  basil, crumbled
¼ cup orzo (rice-shaped
  macaroni for soup,
  also called
  "soupettes")
Salt and pepper

In a medium skillet, brown sausage, breaking it up in small pieces
as it cooks. Remove from skillet with a slotted spoon; place in a
large saucepan.

Sauté onion in sausage drippings until tender. Remove onion with
a slotted spoon; add to sausage. Add vegetables, chicken broth,
and sweet basil to sausage mixture. Bring soup to a boil; stir well.

Cook over moderate heat 15 minutes. Stir in orzo and salt and
pepper to taste. Reduce heat to low; simmer covered 20 minutes
or until orzo is tender. Serves 4.

boeuf (beef) bourguignonne

2 pounds cubed beef
3 to 4 carrots, cut up
1 cup chopped celery
2 onions, sliced
2 cups canned tomatoes
1 cup tomato sauce
1 clove garlic, mashed
3 tablespoons minute
 tapioca

1 tablespoon sugar
½ cup Burgundy wine
1 cup sliced water
 chestnuts
1 can sliced or chopped
 mushrooms
2 cans small Irish
 potatoes

Combine all ingredients in large casserole except chestnuts, mushrooms, and potatoes. Cook at 250°F 5 hours; during last hour add 1 cup sliced water chestnuts, 1 can sliced or chopped mushrooms, and 2 cans (15¼ ounce) small Irish potatoes. Will freeze. Serves 4 to 6.

japanese beef stew

8 cups beef stock
3 pounds beef stew meat,
 cut into bite-size pieces
4 turnips, quartered
2 carrots, cut into bite-
 size pieces
2 cans water chestnuts,
 sliced if desired
10 small potatoes,
 peeled and left whole

Salt to taste
Freshly ground black
 pepper to taste
2 tablespoons soy sauce
4 stalks celery, cut into
 1-inch pieces
10 small white onions
4 scallions, cut into ½-
 inch pieces

Bring beef stock to a boil; add all ingredients except celery, white onions, and scallions. Simmer 30 minutes; add celery and onions; simmer until meat is tender. Add scallions; simmer 2 minutes more.

Serve stew with rice, if desired. Serves 6.

43

italian lamb stew

2 pounds lamb neck or
  shoulder slices
2 tablespoons vegetable
  oil
1 small onion, sliced
1 clove of garlic, pressed
1 20-ounce can tomatoes
1½ teaspoons salt
¼ teaspoon oregano
  leaves
⅛ teaspoon ground
  pepper
1 bay leaf
2 medium zucchini
¼ pound small
  mushrooms, sliced
1 20-ounce can white
  kidney beans
½ cup small pitted ripe
  olives

italian lamb stew

Brown lamb in the oil in a heavy Dutch oven. Pour off any excess drippings; add onion, garlic, tomatoes, salt, oregano, pepper and bay leaf. Cover; simmer 45 minutes. Remove bay leaf.

Cut zucchini into ½-inch slices; add to lamb mixture. Stir in mushrooms. Cook 15 minutes longer or until vegetables and lamb are tender.

Drain kidney beans; add to lamb mixture. Add olives; cook about 5 minutes longer. Serves 8.

albanian lamb stew

1 pound lean lamb, cut
  into ¾-inch cubes
  (boneless shoulder or
  leg of lamb may be
  used)
2 tablespoons vegetable
  oil

1 cup water
2 eggs
1 cup plain yogurt
½ teaspoon salt

Brown cubed lamb in hot vegetable oil in a large skillet. Add water; simmer, uncovered, until water has evaporated, about 20 to 25 minutes.

Place browned cubes in a greased, shallow, 1-quart casserole dish.

Beat together eggs, yogurt, and salt. Pour over meat. Bake at 350°F 20 minutes or until golden brown.

Serve stew at once with a tossed salad containing black olives, lettuce, onions, tomatoes, and perhaps some feta cheese. Serves 4.

note
Lean beef, chuck or round, may be substituted for lamb in this recipe to reduce costs. Individual ramekins may be used in place of a single casserole dish.

creamed vegetable stew

1 cup diced carrots
1 cup cubed potatoes
½ cup diced green sweet
    pepper
½ cup sliced green onions
1 tomato, peeled and
    chopped

1 cup diced celery
Salt
½ pound salt pork
½ cup all-purpose flour
4 cups milk

Place carrots, potatoes, green pepper, onions and celery in a large saucepan; add 2 teaspoons of salt and enough water to cover vegetables. Bring to a boil, then reduce heat; simmer until vegetables are tender. Drain; set aside.

Wash salt pork; remove rind. Cut salt pork into cubes; place in a large saucepan. Cook over medium heat until cubes are brown, stirring frequently.

Add flour; mix well. Stir in milk; bring just to a boil, stirring constantly. Reduce heat; simmer until mixture is thickened. Season with salt to taste. Add vegetables; heat through. Serves 8.

note
It is important that the mixture not be boiled hard after milk has been added to prevent scalding the mixture. When vegetables are added to pork, the stew should be maintained at a simmer to prevent vegetables from becoming mushy.

creamed vegetable stew

steak and vegetable stew

1 1½-pound boneless round steak
3 tablespoons butter
3 tablespoons vegetable oil
4 green onions, thinly sliced
8 round radishes, thinly sliced
½ cup diced green or red sweet pepper
1½ cups thinly sliced onions
1½ cups thinly sliced cabbage
1 Bouquet Garni (see Index)
Salt and freshly ground pepper to taste

Remove all of fat from steak; cut steak into small cubes. Melt butter with oil in a large skillet over high heat. Add steak; cook, stirring constantly, until steak loses red color. Remove from skillet with a slotted spoon; place in a large casserole. Reduce heat under skillet to medium, then add vegetables to butter mixture remaining in skillet; cook, stirring constantly, until wilted.

Turn into casserole and add Bouquet Garni, salt and pepper. Add enough boiling water to cover all ingredients, then cover casserole.

Bake in a preheated 325°F oven 1 rack below center about 3 hours or until steak is tender. Remove Bouquet Garni; skim grease from top of casserole. The liquid may be thickened with cornstarch, if desired. Serve with French bread. Stew may be chilled after baking and fat removed from top, then reheated. Serves 6.

steak and vegetable stew

lamb stew I

1 tablespoon vegetable oil
1 pound boneless lamb, cut in 1-inch cubes
1 tablespoon flour
1 teaspoon salt
1/4 teaspoon pepper
1 cup white wine
1 tablespoon tomato paste
2 cups water
1 clove garlic, minced
1/2 pound carrots, cubed
2 turnips, cubed
1/4 pound fresh green beans, trimmed
6 small potatoes, peeled and quartered
6 small whole onions, peeled
1/4 pound fresh green peas

Heat oil in a 2-quart saucepan. Brown lamb well on all sides. Sprinkle with flour, salt, and pepper; stir well to coat lamb. Add wine, tomato paste, water, and garlic. Bring to a simmer; cover; cook 40 minutes.
Add all vegetables except peas. Cover; cook slowly about 30 minutes, until lamb is tender and vegetables are done. Add peas; cook 8 minutes or until done. Serves 4.

lamb stew II

1 tablespoon olive oil
2 tablespoons butter or margarine
1 1/4 pounds lamb for stew, cut in 1 1/2-inch cubes
1 medium onion, quartered and separated into sections
1 cup tomato puree
1/2 cup white wine
1/4 cup water
1/2 teaspoon oregano
1/2 teaspoon salt
1/4 teaspoon pepper
3 carrots, peeled and sliced
1 medium zucchini, sliced
1/2 of a 9-ounce package frozen cut green beans

Measure oil and butter or margarine into a heavy skillet or 3-quart saucepan; place over medium-high heat until butter melts. Add lamb; brown on all sides.

Remove lamb from pan; add onion; cook until limp. Add tomato puree, wine, water, oregano, salt, pepper, carrots, and browned meat; mix well. Reduce heat to simmer; cook 1 1/2 hours or until the lamb is tender. Add zucchini and green beans.

Cook 30 minutes more or until the vegetables are tender. Serves 4.

free-to-be stew

1 pound ground beef
1 onion, chopped
2 small carrots, sliced
3 small potatoes, cubed
1 1-pound can tomatoes
1 tomato can of water
Salt and pepper to taste

Brown ground beef in skillet; pour off fat.

Add all remaining ingredients; cover; simmer about 1 hour or until vegetables are done. Serves 3 to 4.

boiled beef with chicken and vegetables

2 pounds beef chuck or
　rump roast
2 teaspoons salt
2 medium onions, stuck
　with 3 cloves each
6 carrots, peeled and cut
　in half
4 stalks celery (with leaves)
8 cups beef broth
4 sprigs parsley
1 bay leaf
½ teaspoon thyme
2 cloves garlic
8 peppercorns
1 2- to 3-pound chicken,
　whole or selected
　pieces
½ head cabbage, cut in
　wedges
4 turnips or potatoes,
　peeled and quartered

In large Dutch oven or roaster (at least 5-quart) place beef, salt, onions, 2 carrots, celery, and broth.

Make a bouquet garni by tying parsley, bay leaf, thyme, garlic, and peppercorns in cheesecloth. Add to stew. Simmer gently 1 hour. If using a whole chicken, add to meat after 1 hour cooking; cook ½ hour more. Add vegetables. If using chicken pieces, cook beef 1½ hours, then add chicken and remaining vegetables. After adding vegetables, cook 30 to 45 minutes longer, until vegetables are done and beef is tender. Remove bouquet garni.

To serve, place broth in soup bowls. Serve as a first course, with rice or noodles if desired. Place meat, chicken, and vegetables on a large platter. Pour over a small amount of broth. Serve. Serves 8.

groundnut stew

1 2- to 3-pound frying
　chicken, cut into small
　pieces
Salt and pepper to taste
1 pound beef cubes,
　1-inch size
2 tablespoons oil
　(peanut oil is good)
1 teaspoon salt
1 cup chopped onions
1 green pepper, chopped
2 large tomatoes, peeled
　and diced
1½ teaspoons cayenne
2 cups water
1½ cups peanut butter

Season chicken with salt and pepper; set aside.

Brown beef cubes in hot oil in large skillet. Add salt, ½ the onions, ½ the pepper and tomatoes, cayenne, and water. Simmer this gently for 30 minutes.

Mix 1 cup cooking liquid with peanut butter to make a smooth paste. Add to skillet; cook 15 minutes more. Add chicken pieces and remainder of vegetables. Simmer 30 minutes more, until all is tender. Serves 8 to 10.

onion and beef stew

1¼ pounds stew beef,
  cut in 1-inch pieces
¼ cup olive oil
2 cups sliced onions or 2
  cups small pearl
  onions, peeled
2 cloves garlic, minced
½ teaspoon salt
½ teaspoon pepper
½ teaspoon allspice
½ teaspoon sugar
1 2-inch piece cinnamon
  stick
1⅓ cups dry red wine
1 8-ounce can tomato
  sauce

Brown meat in hot olive oil in a heavy skillet. Remove meat from pan.

Brown onions and garlic. Add other ingredients; stir well. Add browned meat; bring mixture to a boil. Reduce heat to simmer; cover. Cook, stirring occasionally, 2 hours or until meat is very tender.

Serve with macaroni and a green salad. Serves 4.

note
This stew can easily be done in your slow cooker. Brown meat; combine with other ingredients; cook on low heat as manufacturer directs for any stew.

brunswick stew

2 tablespoons oil
1 chicken, jointed
3 to 4 green onions,
  chopped
1 can (about 15 ounces)
  tomatoes
1 package frozen (or 1
  can) whole-kernel corn
1 package frozen (or 1
  pound fresh) green
  beans
1½ cups chicken
  bouillon
1 bay leaf
½ teaspoon powdered
  thyme
1 small can (about 8
  ounces) new potatoes

Preheat oven to 350°F. Heat oil in a sauté pan; brown chicken pieces and onions; remove to a casserole.

Add all other ingredients except potatoes. Drain potatoes; brown in the oil left in sauté pan; add to casserole.

Cover; cook 1 to 1¼ hours. Serve with a tossed salad. Serves 4.

note
This is an all year round casserole of chicken, as good use can be made of canned or frozen vegetables. If you like rabbit, it can be prepared in same way.

hungarian beef goulash

1½ pounds lean beef (chuck or round), cut into 1-inch cubes
2 tablespoons vegetable oil
2 medium onions, chopped
½ teaspoon salt
2 tablespoons paprika
1 cup beef broth
2 green peppers, cubed
2 red peppers (ripe green peppers), cubed
½ cup plain yogurt mixed until smooth with 1 tablespoon all-purpose flour

Brown beef cubes on all sides in hot vegetable oil in a large skillet. Add onions, salt, paprika, and broth. Cover; simmer gently about 2 hours or until meat is very tender.

Add peppers last 10 minutes of cooking. Remove lid so most of cooking liquid can evaporate.

Add yogurt; stir only to distribute it lightly. Serve at once. Serves 4 to 5.

veal with vegetables

2 tablespoons flour
3 tablespoons Kafaloteri or Parmesan cheese
½ teaspoon salt
¼ teaspoon pepper
¼ teaspoon nutmeg
1 egg, beaten
½ cup milk
1 pound thinly sliced leg of veal, cut into serving-size pieces
Flour
6 tablespoons butter
1 eggplant, 1½ pounds
2 tablespoons olive oil
4 tomatoes, peeled and quartered
Salt and pepper
½ teaspoon rosemary
Juice of 1 lemon
2 tablespoons chopped parsley

Combine flour, cheese, salt, pepper, and nutmeg. Add egg and milk; beat until well-blended.

Wipe veal with a damp cloth; dredge in flour. Melt 3 tablespoons of butter in a skillet until it sizzles. Dip veal in flour and egg batter. Fry in butter until golden. Turn and fry other side. Remove to a platter; keep it warm.

Trim stem and cap from eggplant. Leaving skin on eggplant, slice it ¼ inch thick. Pour boiling water over eggplant; let stand a few minutes. Drain.

Heat oil in a medium-size skillet. Add eggplant and tomatoes, salt and pepper to taste, and rosemary. Steam 10 minutes or until eggplant is tender. Stir several times.

Arrange vegetables in a serving dish. Arrange veal on top of vegetables.

Melt remaining butter in pan in which veal was cooked until it foams. Add lemon juice and parsley. Pour over veal. Serve with rice. Serves 4.

Picture on opposite page: veal with vegetables

norwegian stew

1½ cups raw beef, diced
½ pound fresh pork, diced
1½ cups cooked corned
  beef, diced
4 cups raw potatoes, cut
  in small pieces

1 onion, diced
About 2 cups beef stock
1 teaspoon salt
½ teaspoon freshly
  ground pepper

Slowly cook raw beef and pork ½ hour with enough stock to cover. Add rest of ingredients; let simmer at least another hour.

When meat is tender, stew is ready to serve. Serves 4.

ham and vegetable stew

4 or 5 raw carrots, cubed
4 white turnips, cubed
1 pound fresh peas
Salt
1 slice cooked ham or 2
  cups diced leftover ham

1 tablespoon flour
1 tablespoon butter
Chopped parsley for
  garnish

Cook carrots and turnips with peas in salted water to cover. Add diced ham to vegetables and water in which they have been cooked, reserving ¼ cup of vegetable water.

Mix flour and butter with reserved vegetable water. Add this mixture to thicken stew slightly.

Before serving, garnish with chopped parsley. Serves 4 to 6.

mediterranean beef stew

3 pounds beef chuck, cut
  into 1½-inch cubes
¼ cup brandy
½ cup orange juice
4 slices bacon
2 cups sliced onions
3 carrots, peeled and
  sliced ⅛ inch thick
1 1-pound can tomatoes
½ teaspoon salt

⅛ teaspoon pepper
¼ cup chopped parsley
⅛ teaspoon thyme
2 bay leaves
3 cloves garlic, peeled
1 cup red wine
2 small eggplants
1 teaspoon salt
2 tablespoons vegetable
  oil

Place beef in large covered dish. Pour brandy and orange juice over meat; marinate 3 hours.

In Dutch oven sauté bacon to extract some fat. Add onions; sauté until onions are limp. Add meat, marinade, and remaining ingredients except eggplants, 1 teaspoon salt, and oil. Bring to simmer; cover; place in preheated 325°F oven. Bake 1½ hours.

Meanwhile, remove stem and blossom ends of eggplants. Peel, if desired; slice about ½ inch thick. Sprinkle with 1 teaspoon salt. Toss to coat thoroughly. Let stand 45 minutes. Dry with paper towels.

Heat oil in frying pan. Cook eggplant until lightly browned. Add to meat mixture. Bake ½ hour more or until meat is tender. Remove garlic and bay leaves. Serve with parslied potatoes. Serves 6.

vegetable stew with lobster

1 10-ounce package
   frozen cauliflower
1 10-ounce package
   frozen baby carrots
1 10-ounce package
   frozen white or green
   asparagus tips
1 10-ounce package
   frozen peas
2 tablespoons butter
2 tablespoons all-
   purpose flour
1½ cups reserved cooking
   liquid from vegetables

¼ teaspoon nutmeg
Salt and pepper to taste
4 or 5 ounces canned
   black Chinese
   mushrooms, drained
½ cup plain yogurt
8 to 16 ounces cooked
   lobster meat, cut into
   bite-size pieces
Chopped fresh parsley
   leaves

Cook cauliflower, carrots, asparagus, and peas according to package directions. Drain, reserving and combining cooking liquids.

Melt butter in a large saucepan. Stir in flour to make a smooth paste. Gradually stir in 1½ cups of reserved vegetable cooking liquids. Continue to heat; stir until mixture comes to a boil and is thickened. Add nutmeg, salt and pepper. Add cooked vegetables and mushrooms; heat through. Just before serving, stir in yogurt.

Garnish stew with lobster and parsley. Serve at once. Serves 6.

vegetable stew with lobster

korma stew

3 pounds boneless leg of
  lamb
1 cup yogurt
2½ teaspoons salt
1 tablespoon curry powder
6 tablespoons olive oil
1 cup chopped onions
1 clove garlic, pressed
1 teaspoon dry mustard
½ teaspoon freshly
  ground pepper
¼ teaspoon cayenne
  pepper
½ teaspoon ginger
¼ teaspoon cinnamon
⅛ teaspoon cloves
1½ cups water
1 tablespoon lemon
  juice
¼ cup flaked coconut

Trim any fat from lamb; cut lamb into 1-inch cubes. Combine yogurt, salt and curry powder in a mixing bowl. Stir in lamb; marinate at least 2 hours.

Heat 3 tablespoons of oil in a skillet. Add lamb; brown well. Drain off any excess oil. Sauté onions and garlic in remaining oil in a separate skillet until tender. Stir in mustard, pepper, cayenne pepper and spices; cook 2 minutes.

Add lamb; cover tightly; simmer 20 minutes. Pour in water, stirring well. Cover; simmer 30 minutes or until the lamb is tender, adding water, if necessary. Add lemon juice and coconut just before serving. Serve over rice, if desired. Serves 6.

meatball and vegetable skillet stew

1 pound lean ground
  beef
1 egg, slightly beaten
5 tablespoons packaged
  dry bread crumbs
¼ cup milk
2 tablespoons finely
  chopped parsley
1½ teaspoons salt
¼ teaspoon pepper
3 tablespoons salad oil
3 tablespoons flour
1 can (10½ ounces) beef
  broth
¼ teaspoon dried leaf
  basil
1½ cups thinly sliced
  carrots
1½ cups thinly sliced
  celery
4 medium white onions,
  peeled and quartered
2 ripe tomatoes,
  quartered

In large bowl, combine beef, egg, bread crumbs, milk, parsley, 1 teaspoon salt and pepper; mix thoroughly. Shape into 16 one-inch meatballs. Heat oil over medium heat in large skillet; brown meatballs on all sides. Remove from skillet; set aside.

Stir flour into skillet; blend well. Slowly add broth, ½ teaspoon salt and basil. Cook, stirring occasionally, until mixture is slightly thickened. Add carrots, celery and onion. Cover. Cook 20 minutes, or until vegetables are almost tender. Add meatballs and tomatoes; cover. Cook 15 minutes longer, or until vegetables are tender. Serves 4.

fast fish dinner

2 cups canned tomatoes,
  drained (1-pound can)
2 tablespoons butter or
  margarine
1½ cups diced celery
2 medium onions, sliced
1 pound frozen fish fillets,
  cut into bite-size pieces

1 teaspoon salt
¼ teaspoon black
  pepper
2 cups canned potatoes,
  drained and sliced
Parsley for garnish

Put drained tomatoes and butter in medium skillet; bring to a boil. Add celery and onions; simmer until onions are soft, 3 to 5 minutes. Add fish, salt, pepper, and potatoes, stirring once. Cover skillet; simmer this 10 minutes.

Garnish with parsley, and serve. Serves 4.

lamb pilaf

1 onion, chopped
1 tablespoon water
1 tablespoon dry
  vermouth
¼ teaspoon allspice
¼ teaspoon cinnamon
¼ teaspoon thyme
2 cups cooked lamb, cut
  in ½-inch cubes
3 cups cooked rice
1 tomato, peeled and
  chopped

1 cup cooked sliced
  zucchini
⅓ cup pine nuts or
  slivered almonds
⅓ cup raisins, soaked in
  hot water for 5 min-
  utes and drained
1 cup beef broth or
  bouillon

In a large frypan, cook onion in water and vermouth until translucent. Stir in spices; cook 1 minute. Add all the remaining ingredients; cook over medium heat 15 minutes. Stir frequently. Serve hot. Serves 6.

lamb stew with noodles

2 pounds boneless leg of
  lamb
¼ cup olive oil
1 2-ounce can anchovy
  fillets
½ teaspoon basil
1 teaspoon grated lemon
  rind
1 clove of garlic, pressed

2 tablespoons white
  wine vinegar
½ teaspoon freshly
  ground pepper
1 cup beef consommé
2 teaspoons cornstarch
2 tablespoons cold water
3 cups cooked noodles

Trim any fat and membrane from lamb; cut lamb into 1-inch cubes. Heat oil in a heavy skillet. Add lamb; cook over medium heat until well browned. Drain off excess oil.

Drain anchovy fillets; cut into small pieces. Add anchovy pieces, basil, lemon rind, garlic, vinegar, pepper and consommé to lamb; cover. Simmer about 1 hour or until lamb is tender, adding boiling water, if needed, to keep liquid measurement at 1 cup.

Combine cornstarch and 2 tablespoons of cold water, stirring to blend. Stir cornstarch mixture into stew; cook, stirring constantly, until thickened. You may serve this over noodles. Serves 6.

1½ cups minced onions
¼ pound mushrooms, sliced
2 tablespoons vegetable oil
1 pound lean ground beef
1 cup beef broth
⅝ teaspoon nutmeg
½ teaspoon Worcestershire sauce
1 teaspoon salt
½ teaspoon pepper
3 medium potatoes
3 tablespoons butter
2 eggs
4 tart apples
½ cup fine dry bread crumbs

In a frypan sauté onions and mushrooms in vegetable oil until soft. Add ground beef; sauté mixture 3 to 4 minutes. Stir in broth; bring to a simmer. Add ½ teaspoon nutmeg, Worcestershire sauce, ½ teaspoon salt, and ¼ teaspoon pepper.

Peel potatoes; boil them in salted water until tender, about 30 minutes. Drain; put through a food mill or grinder. Beat in 2 tablespoons butter, ½ teaspoon salt, and ¼ teaspoon pepper. Adjust seasonings to taste. Beat in eggs and remaining nutmeg.

Peel, core, and slice apples. Layer mixtures in a 1½-quart buttered baking dish. Spread ⅓ of potatoes on bottom of dish. Top with ½ of the meat mixture and ½ of the apples. Continue with layers, ending with a layer of potatoes. Sprinkle top with bread crumbs; dot with remaining butter. Bake at 375°F 45 minutes, then at 400°F 10 minutes more. Serves 4.

6 cups thinly sliced cabbage (about 2 pounds)
1 1-pound, 12-ounce can sauerkraut
1½ teaspoons salt
2 bay leaves
8 pork loin chops
1½ cups water
1 pound smoked sausage or frankfurters, sliced ½ inch thick
2 8-ounce cans tomato sauce

hunter's stew with cabbage

Spread cabbage in bottom of a large roaster. Cover with sauerkraut. Sprinkle with salt. Add bay leaves. Place pork chops on top; add water. Cover; bake at 325°F 1 hour. Add sausage and tomato sauce. Continue baking until meat is tender.

Serve with boiled potatoes. Serves 8.

romanian lamb stew

3 pounds boned lamb
   shoulder
6 tablespoons olive oil
2 medium green sweet
   peppers
1/2 pound green beans
1 small eggplant
3/4 pound yellow squash

1 cup sliced onions
1 cup sliced okra
3 medium tomatoes,
   sliced
2 teaspoons salt
1 teaspoon paprika
Cayenne pepper to taste

Trim any fat from lamb; cut lamb into 1-inch cubes. Heat 3 table-spoons of the oil in a skillet. Add lamb; cook, stirring frequently, until browned.

Cut green peppers into strips. Trim the ends from beans; cut beans into small pieces. Peel eggplant; cut into cubes. Cut off ends of squash; cut squash into cubes. Heat remaining oil in a large saucepan. Add onions, green peppers, eggplant, squash, beans and okra; sauté until vegetables are lightly browned.

Place alternate layers of lamb, sautéed vegetables and tomato slices in a casserole, sprinkling each layer with salt, paprika and cayenne pepper. Bake, covered, in a preheated 350°F oven 1 hour or until the lamb is tender. Serves 8.

irish stew

3 pounds lamb
2 tablespoons vegetable
   oil
4 large onions, coarsely
   chopped
8 large potatoes, cut into
   cubes
1 1/2 cups boiling water
1/2 teaspoon hot sauce
1 teaspoon salt
2 whole cloves
Flour

Cut lamb into cubes; remove any fat or membranes.

Heat oil in deep, heavy skillet. Add lamb; brown well. Add onions, potatoes, water, hot sauce, salt, and cloves. Cover skillet; simmer 2 hours, adding more boiling water, if needed, to keep liquid at same level. Remove cloves. Drain liquid from skillet; measure. Pour into large saucepan; bring to boil.

Mix 1 tablespoon flour and 1 tablespoon water together for each cup of liquid; blend well. Stir into boiling liquid. Cook, stirring constantly, until thickened. Pour back into skillet; heat through. Serves 8.

broth
**1 large fish head
1 bay leaf
1 medium onion,
    chopped
½ teaspoon salt
¼ teaspoon white
    pepper
6 cups water**

stew
**1 large onion, chopped
1 clove garlic, minced
1 tablespoon white wine
1 tablespoon water
3 medium potatoes,
    peeled and cubed
1 pound whitefish fillets,
    cut into cubes
2 tablespoons lemon
    juice
3 medium tomatoes,
    peeled and chopped
¼ cup stuffed green
    olives
1 tablespoon capers
Salt and white pepper to
    taste
Chopped parsley for
    garnish**

In a 4-quart saucepan, combine ingredients for broth; simmer 1 hour. Strain; reserve broth.

Meanwhile, cook onion and garlic in wine and water until soft. Add fish broth and potatoes; simmer 30 minutes.

While potatoes are cooking, sprinkle fish with lemon juice; add to broth 10 minutes before end of cooking time. After 5 minutes add tomatoes, olives, and capers. Season stew to taste; sprinkle with chopped parsley. Serves 4.

**fish with
vegetables and
yogurt**

**1 onion, sliced
1 green pepper, sliced
1 tomato, peeled and
    chopped
1¼ pounds fish fillets
1 clove garlic, minced**

**½ teaspoon oregano
½ teaspoon salt
¼ teaspoon pepper
3 tablespoons butter
1 cup plain yogurt or
    sour cream**

Place half of the vegetables on bottom of a greased baking dish. Top with fish fillets. Sprinkle with garlic, oregano, salt, and pepper. Top with remaining vegetables; dot with butter. Bake at 350°F 30 minutes.

Top dish with yogurt; cook 10 minutes more. Serves 4.

chicken-pepper stew

chicken-pepper stew

1 3-pound broiler-fryer
5 large carrots
1 tablespoon salt
5 white peppercorns
5 whole allspice
1 bay leaf
3 whole cloves
1 leek, chopped
2 large onions, chopped

2 cups shredded
  cabbage
1 6-ounce can tomato
  puree (optional)
½ teaspoon minced chili
  pepper
1 cup ground peanuts
1 cup boiled rice

Place chicken in a large saucepan; add enough water to cover. Bring to a boil; skim well.

Dice 1 carrot; add to chicken with salt, peppercorns, allspice, bay leaf, cloves and leek. Cook about 40 minutes or until chicken is tender. Remove chicken from broth; cool. Strain broth; add enough water, if needed, to make 4 cups liquid. Reserve ½ cup broth for later use; pour remaining broth back into saucepan.

Grate remaining carrots; add to broth with onions, cabbage, tomato puree and chili pepper. Bring to a boil; reduce heat. Cook, stirring frequently, until thickened and vegetables are tender. Add peanuts; cook 15 minutes longer, stirring frequently.

Remove skin and bones from chicken; cut chicken into large pieces. Combine reserved broth with chicken in a heavy saucepan; heat through. Place chicken, vegetable mixture and rice in separate serving dishes. Place rice, then chicken, then vegetable mixture in soup bowls to serve. Serves 6.

1 pound veal, cut into
   1-inch pieces
2 strips bacon, chopped
2 tablespoons vegetable
   oil
1 large onion, chopped
1 clove garlic, minced
1 green pepper, cut into
   strips
2 carrots, peeled and
   sliced

2 tomatoes, peeled and
   quartered
½ teaspoon salt
2 cups beef bouillon
½ teaspoon paprika
¼ teaspoon black
   pepper
¾ cup long-grained rice
3 sprigs parsley,
   chopped

In a 4-quart Dutch oven, sauté veal and bacon in hot oil. Remove; reserve meats.

Sauté onion, garlic, and green pepper strips in same pot. Return meats; add carrots, tomatoes, salt, bouillon, paprika, pepper, and rice. Cover Dutch oven; place in a preheated 350°F oven for 1½ hours. Check liquid after 1 hour; add ¼ cup water if necessary. Before serving, sprinkle with parsley. Serves 4.

note
This recipe may be cooked in any ovenproof casserole in place of a Dutch oven.

marinade
1 cup chopped onions
½ cup chopped carrot
½ cup chopped celery
1 clove garlic, minced
2 whole cloves
¼ teaspoon rosemary
¼ teaspoon thyme
1 bay leaf

6 cranberries
5 peppercorns
1 tablespoon chopped
   parsley
½ teaspoon salt
3 cups dry red wine
¼ cup red wine vinegar
½ cup vegetable oil

stew
3 pounds venison stew
   meat
½ teaspoon marjoram
¼ cup butter or
   margarine

1 cup chopped onions
¼ cup flour
1 cup beef broth
¼ teaspoon pepper
1 cup sour cream

Place marinade ingredients into 2-quart saucepan. Bring to boil. Reduce heat; simmer 10 minutes. Cool.

Put venison and marjoram in large casserole. Pour cooled marinade over meat; cover. Refrigerate 24 hours; stir occasionally. Drain meat; reserve marinade. Pat meat dry.

Melt butter in large saucepan. When hot, add meat. Brown; stir to prevent burning. Remove meat; brown 1 cup onions. Stir in flour; mix until well blended. Add broth and 2 cups reserved marinade. Add pepper. Bring stew to boil; stir until slightly thickened. Add meat; cover. Simmer about 1 hour, until meat is tender. Skim off fat. Add sour cream; heat through. Serves 8.

bouillabaisse

bouillabaisse

1 pound mackerel fillets
½ pound halibut fillets
1 pound flounder fillets
4 medium tomatoes, skinned
4 medium potatoes
3 cloves garlic
1 leek, sliced
2 sprigs of parsley
1 bay leaf
1 teaspoon grated lemon rind

6 cups boiling water
1½ teaspoons salt
Freshly ground pepper to taste
¼ cup dry white wine
½ teaspoon saffron or 1½ tablespoons turmeric
5 thick slices of bread
1 tablespoon olive oil

Cut fish fillets into bite-size pieces. Cut tomatoes into wedges. Peel and slice potatoes. Combine fish fillets, tomatoes and potatoes in a soup kettle. Crush 1 clove of garlic; add to kettle; add leek, parsley, bay leaf and lemon rind. Pour 6 cups of boiling water into kettle; add salt, pepper and wine.

Bring to a boil; cook about 20 minutes or until fish flakes easily when tested with a fork.

Crush remaining 2 cloves of garlic; blend in saffron. Remove crust from 1 slice of bread; soak bread in a small amount of water. Squeeze water from the bread; mix bread with garlic mixture. Add oil and ¼ cup of stock from fish mixture and mix well. Spread oil mixture over remaining bread slices; place slices in 4 soup bowls. Ladle soup over bread slices. Serves 4.

carrot stew

1 pound carrots
½ pound leeks or celery
2 tablespoons vegetable oil
1 cup dry white wine
½ teaspoon salt
¼ teaspoon white pepper
½ pound ground veal
½ teaspoon Worcestershire sauce
2 sprigs parsley, chopped

Clean and peel carrots; cut into 1-inch strips. Clean leeks or celery; slice crosswise into ½-inch pieces.

Heat 1 tablespoon oil in a medium saucepan; lightly stir-fry carrots and leeks (or celery) 3 minutes. Add wine, salt, and pepper; cover saucepan; simmer 30 minutes.

Meanwhile, brown ground veal in 1 tablespoon hot oil about 5 minutes. Add meat to cooked vegetables. Stir in Worcestershire sauce; adjust seasonings. Serve on a preheated dish; garnish with chopped parsley. Serves 4.

beef stew mexican-style

**beef stew
mexican-style**

**1½ pounds lean stewing
beef, cut into cubes
1 large onion, sliced
1 clove garlic, minced
4 tablespoons olive oil
3 tablespoons wine vinegar
½ cup tomato sauce**

**1 cup red wine
1 bay leaf
1 teaspoon oregano
½ teaspoon salt
¼ teaspoon pepper
1 7-ounce can green chili
salsa**

**beer rice
2 tablespoons olive oil
1 cup raw long-grain rice
1 10¾-ounce can con-
densed onion soup**

**1 10¾-ounce soup can
of beer**

Combine all stew ingredients in large saucepan. Bring mixture to a
boil, stirring occasionally. Reduce heat to simmer; cook 3 hours or
until meat falls apart. Serve with Beer Rice. Serves 4.

To make Beer Rice, heat olive oil in medium saucepan over
moderate heat. Add rice; brown lightly, stirring constantly. Add
onion soup and beer. Cover tightly; simmer 20 to 25 minutes or
until all liquid is absorbed. Serves 4.

note
This stew is moderately hot; if you prefer milder food, cut amount
of green chili salsa in half.